RAPPED IN THE FLAG

DAVID WELLS

RAPPED IN THE FLAG

A
Hip-hop Guide
to the American Presidents

Illustrated by Molly Brau

authorHOUSE®

AuthorHouse™ LLC
1663 Liberty Drive
Bloomington, IN 47403
www.authorhouse.com
Phone: 1-800-839-8640

Published by AuthorHouse 05/06/2014

ISBN: 978-1-4969-1057-8 (sc)
ISBN: 978-1-4969-1058-5 (e)

CONTENTS

GEORGE WASHINGTON
"The Father of Our Country"

Listen up, young people, and I'll lay down some facts
'Bout the Father of your country and his awesome acts.

Born in Virginia in colonial days,
Grew up on an estate, learned baronial ways.

His parents taught him values like honesty;
You might know the legend about the cherry tree.

His daddy asked "Who cut it down? I'll find out by and by."
Little George said "Father, I cannot tell a lie."

It wasn't any thief who sneaked in to snatch it.
I must I confess I was the one; I did it with my hatchet."

He learned his lessons well, grew up tall and proud,
Ability and strength made him stand out from the crowd.

Surveyor and soldier, traveled throughout the land;
Frontier life and war helped make him a man.

When the colonies rebelled in 1775,
The army needed leadership in order to survive.

George Washington came forward and accepted the call,
Like a mighty oak, he always stood tall.

With patience to endure, and the courage to dare,
He led his men at night across the Delaware.

The Hessians were drunk and unrepentant,
When Washington attacked that Christmas at Trenton.

His patriots saw victory, but also defeat;
Sometimes in the winter they had little to eat.

At Valley Forge their suffering was really severe.
With Washington beside them, they had to persevere.

At Yorktown he accepted the British surrender;
Independence triumphed, led by Liberty's defender.

Unrivaled hero, they offered him a crown.
Not wanting to be king, he turned it down.

Instead he went home to Mt. Vernon plantation,
Raised tobacco 'till they called him back to save the nation.

Without a better union, the states might divide.
They met in Philadelphia and asked him to preside.

These founding Fathers argued, fussed and compromised,
Produced the best constitution ever devised.

They told old George "Hey, Buddy, you're not quite through,
We'll need a strong president; how about you?"

Reluctantly but willingly he took the oath,
Led the new republic through its early growth.

Appointed brilliant men to the Cabinet and the courts,
Watched as they debated Hamilton's reports.

He favored the plan to repay the national debt.
For this he was roasted in the *National Gazette*.

Dignified but modest, he never put on airs.
Tried to keep us neutral in foreign affairs.

Elected for two terms, he kept the nation united;
His Farewell Address showed he was far-sighted.

He warned us not to fall into partisan strife,
Or to exclude virtue from political life.

We should pay our debts and keep strong in times of peace,
Friends would respect us and our enemies would decrease.

When Washington died, the bells rang from every steeple;
First in war, first in peace, first in the hearts of his people.

JOHN ADAMS
"His Rotundity"

Patriot, founding father, independence leader;
Political philosopher, voracious reader.

Honest and forthright, plain-spoken and blunt;
Never timid in debate, always ready to confront.

Bonny Johnny Adams was short and rather plump;
Ridiculed at times, he was nobody's chump.

Graduated Harvard, owned a farm, practiced law.
Came to the conclusion that the British should withdraw.

Most colonists agreed that self-government was best;
Against the Stamp and Tea Acts, they began to protest.

The Continental Congress met to organize resistance
To British depradations like the Writs of Assistance.

Massachusetts led the fight for an independent nation;
Adams led the group to write the Declaration.

It was Jefferson's words that went down on the page,
But Adams' oratory kept him on center stage.

He urged the Congress to give Washington command;
Raise an army and a navy to defend the homeland.

Before the war was over and independence won,
Adams went to Europe after peace talks had begun.

Ten years of diplomacy, trade talks and a treaty;
Wrote some books and many letters to his sweetie;

Returned to Massachusetts, his home and Abigail,
But when the country called, he served without fail.

Eight years as vice-president, an office too inactive;
At least it helped prepare him for something more attractive.

In 1797 he became president number two,
Relations with France caused a real hullabaloo.

The French hijacked our ships down in the Caribbean;
The daunting tasks of Adams seemed Herculean.

Could he keep the peace with the Federalists crying "War"?
Would the British help us? What about the tsar?

Our diplomats were dissed in the XYZ affair;
Adams built up the navy, but war he did forswear.

Congress overreached, passing acts against sedition;
Adams took advantage to silence the opposition.

The threat of war abated with an overture to France;
Adams acted wisely, but he didn't have a chance

To serve another term when Hamilton opposed him;
After 4 years in office, the electors deposed him.

Spent his last night in office appointing midnight judges;
For years thereafter Jefferson nursed some grudges;

Finally ended their quarrel, it was all just politics;
Both died on July 4th, eighteen twenty-six.

THOMAS JEFFERSON
"THE SAGE OF MONTICELLO"

America, we all recognize, is the land of the free;
Freedom-lovers owe a debt to President number three.

This tall red-haired Virginian, Jefferson was his name,
A giant in our history, he never courted fame.

Philosopher-king, America's Aristotle,
Farmer, founding Father, liberty's apostle.

Republicans and Democrats, we're all his descendants,
The author of the Declaration of Independence.

The Continental Congress said, "Tom, we need a writer,"
He took his trusty quill pen, and pulled an all-nighter.

He said the great truths are self-evident:
Our rights come from God, through His benevolence.

Life, liberty, happiness's pursuit,
Government must protect these rights, or else get the boot.

That awesome declaration was a masterpiece of thought,
It served as inspiration for the patriots who fought.

Once free from Britain, we'd need some institutions
To set up a republic, maybe a constitution.

Madison took up the job, for by circumstance,
Jefferson was in Paris, as minister to France.

They sent him a copy, just to be polite,
He thought it sounded pretty good, needed a Bill of Rights.

The Constitution went to the states, all 13 ratified;
By adding those ten amendments, Jefferson was satisfied.

Washington picked his cabinet, a group that was first-rate,
Jefferson became the first Secretary of State.

He argued with Hamilton, over taxes and the bank;
The two-party system has both of them to thank.

States' rights, land ownership, and freedom of the press;
Let America depend on these and she'll enjoy success.

Preachers paid by taxes? He said we didn't need 'em.
No church should be established in a state with religious freedom.

The election of 1800 made him the president
With Louisiana's purchase, he set a precedent.

More land would make us bigger, this huge new territory,
Expanding U.S. power, democracy and glory.

When England stopped our ships, hijacking men and cargo,
Jefferson responded with that ill-fated Embargo.

He finished up his second term, went home to Monticello,
Never did quit learning, this quite remarkable fellow.

He knew French and Spanish, Latin and Greek,
Ignorant folks today might call him a Geek.

Scientist, architect, expert on the Indians,
He started a great university for the Virginians.

The argument over slavery filled him with dread and fright
Awoke him from his slumbers like a firebell in the night.

Never freed his own slaves, couldn't quite make that leap;
The civil war that followed surely would have made him weep.

Reconciled with John Adams, old foes were friends again;
The spirit of '76 they hoped we'd all regain.

He died in 1826 on the 4th of July,
On his ideas and legacy, Americans still rely.

Wherever men love justice, and liberty still thrives,
They say as John Adams did: "Jefferson still survives."

JAMES MADISON

"FATHER OF THE CONSTITUTION"

Little Jimmy Madison was less than five-foot-six,
But he rose to be a giant in American politics.

Loved books and ideas, finished Princeton in two years;
Joined the Virginia lege, left the farm to the overseers.

Could have stayed to manage his prosperous plantation,
Instead he used his talents to grow a brand new nation.

Elected to the Congress during the Revolution;
Realized the need for a stronger constitution.

The Articles we had made it hard to get things done;
There was no chief executive; most thought we needed one.

Then farmers and debtors rose up with Daniel Shays;
A violent rebellion—a dangerous new phase.

Madison and Washington called delegates to Philly:
Lawyers and educated men, not a single hillbilly.

Madison starred at this Constitutional Convention,
Wrote the Virginia Plan, took notes, paid attention

Arguments, discussions, political debates;
Compromise between the big and small states.

After two months the thing was signed and sealed;
But would it be accepted or would it be repealed?

Don't be satisfied
Until it's ratified.

Take it to the states;
Let's have some more debates.

Published famous essays known as the Federalist papers,
Reflecting thoughts on government by the founders and the shapers.

Parties and factions
Show liberty in action

To forestall future fights
Added a Bill of Rights.

Served his friend Tom Jefferson as Secretary of State;
Grievances with Britain began to accumulate.

In 1809 he became president number four;
British provocations he could not ignore.

They stirred up Indian trouble out in the west;
They hijacked our ships; our sailors were impressed.

Arguments for peace the Federalists had to shelve,
As the nation went to war in the year of 1812.

Our navy was tiny and our army was weak,
The British sent a fleet right up the Chesapeake.

Invaded the capital, set Washington aflame;
The Madisons escaped, but the president took the blame.

Still Fort McHenry held through the perilous fight;
Our banner still waved by the dawn's early light.

Though we added no new land, we still came out ahead;
The U.S. gained prestige, the Federalist party was dead.

Madison served 2 terms, then went home to his estate.
The nation agreed his contributions had been great.

After his death, he received more attention,
When Dolley turned over his notes on the convention.

Proving once again his lasting insights,
Representative government based on human rights.

Good Golly, Miss Dolley! Don't be melancholy!
Yo, Constitution, who's your daddy?
Jimmy Maddy!

JAMES MONROE
"LAST OF THE FOUNDING FATHERS"

The fourth Virginia president was James Monroe;
His energy and vision kept him on the go.

The war for independence called him from his studies;
Risked his life for freedom's sake and for his patriot buddies.

After the war was over, Jefferson taught him law.
While serving in the Congress, the future he foresaw.

Helped write the Northwest Ordinance for settling the west,
Helped buy Louisiana, our destiny manifest.

Like Virginia's Patrick Henry, he opposed the Constitution,
Until the Bill of Rights went in, Madison's contribution.

A Democratic-Republican, his foreign policy stance,
Like Jefferson's and Madison's, often favored France.

The Louisiana Purchase he helped negotiate,
Experienced as a diplomat, named Secretary of State;

Sent on many missions, traveled near and far;
After the British burned the capitol, he became Secretary of War.

When Madison retired, Monroe was his successor;
As president he toured all the states, unlike his predecessor.

Modest in his tastes, sincere and forthright,
His first lady a New Yorker named Elizabeth Kortwright.

Monroe was so popular, so upright in his dealings,
His presidency was known as the Era of Good Feelings.

During his reelection, he lost one electoral vote;
Those who love bipartisanship should really take note.

Policy toward Canada showed his peaceful intentions;
Demilitarized the border with the Rush-Bagot convention.

John Quincy Adams led a cabinet that was able;
Devised that famous Doctrine that Monroe laid on the table.

Europe should not meddle in the Western Hemisphere;
With the little new republics there's no need to interfere.

Independence is the new trend Europe should respect;
Latin American liberty the U.S. will protect.

Since 1823 our foreign policy has grown,
But the Monroe Doctrine is still its cornerstone.

In 1819 Adams expanded our domain,
When he acquired Florida in a treaty with Spain.

Peace and prosperity, territorial growth.
Five new states were added since Monroe first took the oath.

Not as brilliant as some others in his generation;
Monroe still showed good judgment and devotion to the nation.

Signed off on the tariff and the Missouri Compromise;
Left office a success in the people's eyes.

JOHN QUINCY ADAMS

"Old Man Eloquent"

First president in office who was a president's son,
The White House not a place where he could get things done.

John Quincy Adams, our greatest diplomat,
Was wrongly described as an old world plutocrat.

Volunteered for foreign service at the age of fourteen;
Served our man in Moscow, learned the envoy's routine.

Later was our minister to Holland and to Prussia;
Practiced law, taught at Harvard, then was sent back to Russia.

Worked out the agreement the Treaty of Ghent,
Had success in foreign lands, wherever he was sent.

His most effective post was Monroe's secretary of state;
But his record as the president was really second-rate.

The campaign of 1824 was hotly contested.
Chief rival: Andrew Jackson, a man that he detested.

Since no one won an electoral college majority,
The constitution gives the House of Rep's the authority.

Adams won in the House, but many folks would say,
He'd made a corrupt bargain with that rascal Henry Clay.

He laid out lofty goals in his inaugural address:
A national observatory for scientific progress,

Bridges, roads, canals to improve transportation,
A national university to improve education.

But he couldn't work with Congress, he was cold and reserved;
Accomplished little in the office that he felt he deserved.

Defeated after four years, he still had things to prove;
Ran for Congress as ex-prez, an unexpected move.

Served Massachusetts for 8 terms in the House.
Pro-slavery Southerners thought he was a louse.

Known for his audacity, if not for his finesse;
Then one day in Congress he collapsed at his desk.

Patriotic and unselfish, dignified but not snooty;
"Where could death have found him but at the post of duty?"

ANDREW JACKSON
"OLD HICKORY"

Born in the backwoods on the old frontier,
Brash and courageous, he knew no fear.

His temper was short, his manners sometimes crude,
He wore a saber scar from that British army dude.

He never studied much, he was a man of action,
A true American hero, General Andrew Jackson.

He made a lot of enemies, he fought a lot of duels,
Had no use for millionaires, foreigners or fools.

Made money as a lawyer, bought land in Tennessee,
Elected to Congress where he learned democracy.

Restless for action, with energy to expend,
Led troops against the Indians at Horseshoe Bend.

Marched into New Orleans with his Tennessee volunteers,
Recruited men of color and creole buccaneers,

Entrenched themselves in the swamp, dared the British to invade,
Two thousand redcoats fell in their deadly fusillade.

His men called him Old Hickory, because he was tough,
But leading the army was not enough.

He wanted the top spot in the nation,
His campaign for president caused a sensation.

He championed the common folk against the aristocrats;
Led the farmers and workers, and other Democrats.

But John Quincy Adams, flinty and abrupt,
Made a bargain with Clay that many called corrupt.

Though Jackson had a lot of votes, he needed more than half;
So Adams got the White House, Old Hickory got the shaft.

He worked to make his comeback in 1828;
When he won in a landslide, the mob did celebrate.

Invaded the White House, stomped around in muddy boots,
Broke dishes and furniture, those drunk redneck galoots.

But Jackson had a plan to rule, to the victor belong the spoils;
Gave jobs to his supporters, to reward them for their toils.

Shook up his snooty cabinet, after the Peggy Eaton affair;
Vice-President Calhoun quit and took the air.

Calhoun led South Carolina with his doctrine of nullification,
Said "We won't pay that tariff; it's an abomination."

This comes real close to treason, the president observed,
Jackson said "The Union—it must be preserved."

The crisis was averted when they found a compromise,
Jackson's style of leadership was seen as strong and wise.

Ignored John Marshall's verdict, in the Cherokee case;
Did not enforce the order; it was such a disgrace.

Poor old Henry Clay choked back his tears,
When Jackson beat him once again to serve for 4 more years.

He railed against the millionaires, closed down the National Bank;
After he left office, the economy went in the tank.

Hey, diddle diddle, old Nicholas Biddle; what happened to all the money?
Speculation in the west, business was depressed, now wasn't that just too funny?

In 1837, he retired to his plantation,
After more than 30 years of service to his nation.

The Whigs called him a tyrant, an ignorant buffoon;
He always regretted that he never hanged Calhoun.

But if he never wrote a book, or left a lot of quotes,
You've still got to respect someone who got so many votes.

Folks loved Andy Jackson, with his flair for the dramatic,
He opened up the government, and made it democratic.

MARTIN VAN BUREN
"The Little Magician"

A Dutchman from Kinderhook, a clever politician;
Wily New York Democrat, the Little Magician.

Martin Van Buren was Andrew Jackson's boy;
There was nothing about politics that he did not enjoy.

Built the Albany Regency, the first political machine;
Extremely efficient, if not extremely clean.

Served his state as Senator and Governor after that.
Proud to lead the working folks, like any Democrat.

Named to Jackson's cabinet as Secretary of State;
Against John C. Calhoun he provided counterweight.

Later as v.p he presided over the Senate;
Wore pistols just in case there was any trouble in it.

Jackson made it clear that Van Buren should succeed him;
The Whigs could not agree on a candidate to lead them.

So Van Buren was elected prez in 1836;
The economy then broke down with no hope for a fix.

Speculation led to panic as the land boom bubble burst;
Millions lost their money; the poor suffered the worst.

Farm prices fell, factories closed up shop,
Jackson's war against the Bank turned out to be flop.

To many it appeared that Van Buren didn't care;
But he was one who still believed in laissez-faire.

Let the government stay out of the economic game,
No national bank or public works or high taxes to blame.

Times might be hard, but they'd eventually get better;
Government couldn't help things if it became a debtor.

Whigs saw the depression as a campaign issue brewing;
They started to refer to him as "Martin Van Ruin."

The 1840 voters punished Van at the polls.
Put William Henry Harrison at the controls.

It didn't help when Van opposed Texas' annexation;
And that the Seminole war had caused such vexation.

Van Buren tried a comeback but his time had clearly passed;
When Democrats picked Polk, Van Buren was downcast.

The Free Soil folks asked him to lead their third party;
He campaigned eagerly, still hale and hearty.

Carried not a single state nor one electoral vote;
His chance for winning that one was always remote.

Eighteen forty-eight brought an end to his career;
Returned to Kinderhook to live out his last years.

WILLIAM HENRY HARRISON
"OLD TIPPECANOE"

Born in Virginia, he settled in the west;
Wars with the Indians put him to the test.

Defeated Tecumseh at a place called Tippecanoe.
War Hero to Commander-in-chief: a path he would pursue.

For political office he was always ambitious;
His inauguration was less than auspicious.

Served as governor of Indiana territory;
The War of 1812 brought military glory.

Ran for the White House, nominated as a Whig;
The 1840 campaign was loud, bold, and big.

Log Cabin and Hard Cider, incredible ballyhoo;
Their slogan: "Tippecanoe and Tyler, too."

The Dem's put up Van Buren for reelection;
Hard times led the voters to change direction.

The Whigs jeered "Van is a used-up man."
Harrison was elected, but did he have a plan?

Inauguration day was rainy, windy, and cold;
William Henry Harrison was sixty-eight years old.

Daniel Webster cut down his speech, to two hours long;
Harrison delivered every word; his speaking voice was strong.

But in the rain he caught a cold, went home and went to bed.
The cold became pneumonia; in a month he was dead.

Had potential as a leader; his campaign had been clever;
But the Harrison presidency was the shortest ever.

JOHN TYLER
"His Accidency"

Born in Virginia, a Southern aristocrat;
But was he a Whig, or was he a Democrat?

Finished William and Mary while only seventeen;
Had a headstrong personality, a mind that was keen.

Elected to the Senate at the age of thirty-six;
Broke with Andrew Jackson, one of those mavericks.

Believed in state's rights, even nullification;
Resigned from the Senate after an altercation.

The Whigs then recruited him as Harrison's running mate;
"Tippecanoe and Tyler, too" wowed the electorate.

First veep to move up when the president died;
When he used his power, the Whigs were fit to be tied.

Retained Harrison's cabinet, but let them know who's boss;
When he vetoed Clay's bills, the Whigs felt double-crossed.

Everyone but Webster in the cabinet resigned;
Tyler vetoed more bills; he really didn't mind.

The Whigs cajoled and argued, really tried to reach him;
When he turned a deaf ear, they tried to impeach him.

They failed by a vote of eighty-three to twenty-seven;
Some wondered if this president had the mandate of heaven.

An agreement with the British was finally obtained;
Webster signed a treaty, fixed the boundary of Maine.

John Tyler's accomplishments as president may be checkered,
But as a family man there's no doubt he holds the record.

Sired fifteen children, was married twice;
Life in the Tyler White House must have been paradise.

An incumbent without a party in 1844,
Tyler recognized that he'd soon be out the door

The problem of Texas had cried out for solution.
Tyler annexed it through Congressional resolution.

Retired to Virginia, still held his states' rights views;
Then in 1860 came that dangerous news.

Civil War was imminent; he proposed a Peace Convention;
When that conference failed, there was no more intervention.

Like others in Virginia, he accepted secession.
Died before he attending a Confederate session.

JAMES K. POLK
"Young Hickory"

Born in North Carolina, graduated from UNC,
Moved west to practice law in the state of Tennessee.

Elected to Congress, Jacksonian Democrat;
The political arena was his natural habitat.

Speaker of the House, popular with the folk,
Henry Clay wanted to know, "Who is James K. Polk?"

Someone put his name in, hoping Jackson would endorse;
Finally got the nomination as a very Dark Horse;

Beat Clay in a close one in 1844;
Tyler annexed Texas as he went out the door;

Polk entered the White House with expansion on his mind;
California to be added, Oregon's boundary defined.

But Mexico refused to sell New Mexico or California,
Polk just shrugged and muttered, "Don't say we didn't warn ya."

Polk settled with Britain, a skillful compromise;
Oregon's border, though some would criticize.

"Fifty-four-forty or Fight!" had been their battle-cry;
Polk said Forty-nine is fine; we've got other fish to fry.

Mexico was up in arms, sent troops across the border;
Polk defended Texas with a military order.

Asked Congress to declare war amidst the turmoil;
Since "American blood has been shed on American soil."

The victory at Buena Vista was Zachary Taylor's;
Vera Cruz was captured by American sailors.

Outnumbered almost four to one, our troops fought hard and well;
After fifteen months of combat, Mexico City fell.

The treaty of Guadaloupe gave America vast new lands.
New Mexico and California were now in U.S. hands.

Our soldiers had risked life and limb, showed noteworthy bravery,
But Northern politicians claimed the war had been for slavery.

Whig support for the war had been qualified;
Paid $15 million, Mexico was mollified.

Polk then turned to domestic reform:
Lower tariff rates would be the new norm.

The Bank of the U.S. Democrats had shunned;
But an independent treasury could store government funds;

In 4 years James K. Polk accomplished all his goals;
Achieved success in all his presidential roles.

Left office after one term, went home to Tennessee;
Cholera killed him; he died at fifty-three.

ZACHARY TAYLOR
"Old Rough and Ready"

Grew up in Kentucky, fought Tecumseh in Indiana;
Bought a plantation in South Louisiana.

He served in the army for over forty years.
Then the Whigs convinced him that he ought to change careers.

Zachary Taylor, known as Old Rough and Ready,
Decisive in battle, his leadership was steady.

Disliked fancy uniforms, preferred his old clothes;
Liked to stay outdoors, didn't care if he froze.

From the Illinois frontier to the Florida swamp;
He lived a soldier's life, far from pageantry and pomp.

Then at Buena Vista in the Mexican War,
His dramatic victory made him a star.

Though he'd never even voted and no one knew his views,
The Whigs nominated him; how could he refuse?

Avoided most issues while just a candidate,
Elected twelfth president in 1848.

Asked Congress for a tariff to pay off the war debt;
Spoke out against the Southern secessionist threat.

Favored California's admission to the Union;
Looked with disfavor on the talk of disunion.

The year of 1850 saw a compromise proposed.
It had a fugitive slave clause, and Taylor was opposed.

Before he could veto it, fate intervened;
On that hot July 4, a crowd had convened;

For the Washington monument, they laid the cornerstone;
A long ceremony, how the sun had shone!

To keep cool that day Taylor took some bad advice:
Ate cherries and cucumbers, drank milk with ice.

Went home with a stomachache, went straight to bed.
Five days later, the president was dead.

Most likely it was cholera, historians concurred;
But in 1991, his remains were disinterred.

Arsenic poisoning was ruled out by the tests.
Assassination rumors can now be put to rest.

MILLARD FILLMORE

"Doughface"

Grew up in poverty, had an apprenticeship gig,
Went into politics as a New York Whig.

Married a teacher; her name was Abigail;
Learned to read, studied law, determined not to fail.

Elected Vice-president under Old Rough and Ready,
The Whigs' hold on government becoming more unsteady.

An accidental president, Millard Fillmore.
Would he be a leader that the Congress could ignore?

As veep he had presided when the Senate debated;
As prez he would sign or veto what they legislated.

The Compromise of 1850: five different bills
Dealt with slavery, expansion, and sectional ills.

Fillmore signed them in the spirit of conciliation;
Northern critics said it was capitulation.

The South would be aggressive chasing fugitive slaves;
Some would take refuge in northern enclaves.

The law said the feds must help to return them;
Such laws abolitionists said "We will spurn them."

As differing views on slavery collided,
The nation itself became more and more divided.

Harriet Beecher Stowe put in her two cents;
Uncle Tom's Cabin made the South more incensed.

Fillmore was befuddled; there was little he could do;
The Whigs dumped him from their ticket in 1852.

His wife expired, then he retired, went home to Buffalo;
His successors vainly tried to uphold the status quo.

The Civil War was coming, though many would decry it;
Only a Know-Nothing would attempt to deny it.

Though few paid attention, Fillmore still tried to speak;
But the voters recognized his leadership as weak.

Died in 1874, almost totally forgotten;
Remembered for that Compromise, failed and misbegotten.

FRANKLIN PIERCE
"HANDSOME FRANK"

Charming and convivial, they called him Handsome Frank;
When faced with tough decisions, he wavered and he drank.

A Northern politician who pandered to the South,
His leadership in crisis was little more than mouth.

Eighteen-fifties' politics was nothing short of fierce;
The Dem's thought they had found their man in Franklin Pierce.

Congressman then Senator from the Granite State,
He emerged in 1852 as a dark horse candidate.

Friends with Nat Hawthorne from Bowdoin College days,
His military record had earned him little praise.

In Mexico, the story goes, he fell off his horse, then fainted;
They say it was with whiskey that he was too well-acquainted.

The doughface Pierce's party was Southern-dominated;
His poor wife Jane collapsed when he was nominated.

Accepted his election with extreme trepidation;
Then tragedy struck their family on their way to the inauguration.

The train derailed, their son was killed, Jane couldn't stop her tears;
Didn't show herself in public for the next two years.

As president Pierce used every means to catch every fugitive slave;
Against the abolitionists he would often rant and rave.

Signed the Kansas-Nebraska Act; it turned out a disaster;
The nation's plunge toward civil war raced faster and faster.

Pierce told our men in Europe to put pressure on Spain;
Southerners wanted Cuba to add to their domain.

The Ostend Manifesto was a diplomatic mess;
At least the Gadsden Purchase was something like success.

The Whigs were dead but now instead Republicans displaced them.
More and more the Democrats felt Pierce had disgraced them.

The Dem's refused to nominate him for another term;
Picked Old Buck Buchanan their platform to affirm.

The loss of his high office left Pierce in a funk.
He said "There's nothing left now but to get drunk."

Retired to New Hampshire and political isolation;
Opposed the Union effort, denounced emancipation.

Drank even more after Jane passed away;
Shunned, bitter, and lonely, to his dying day.

JAMES BUCHANAN
"Old Buck"

Born in a log cabin, 1812 vet;
His failures in the White House, historians can't forget.

James "Old Buck" Buchanan, doughface Democrat,
Pennsylvania lawyer, Senator, diplomat.

Jackson, Polk, and Pierce had all sent him abroad;
His Ostend Manifesto few did applaud.

Put Spain on notice, they'd have to give up Cuba.
Did the Dutch get nervous about losing Aruba?

The motive was the South's desire to extend slavery;
Their threats and machinations were somewhat unsavory.

Buchanan was elected prez in 1856,
A pro-South Yankee in sectional politics.

Though slavery might be wrong, the constitution does protect it;
As president he believed he could do nothing to correct it.

Irresolute and feckless; let's just see what history brings;
"What's right and what's practical are two different things."

Panic hit in '57, he did nothing about it.
Laissez-faire had worked before, what Democrat could doubt it?

The Dred Scott decision was a blow to freedom's cause;
Buchanan knew his duty was to carry out the laws.

He tried to admit Kansas as a slave state;
The anti-slavery activists he did infuriate.

John Brown's raid set the nation aflame;
Some thought he was a hero; others vilified his name.

Buchanan lacked good judgment, moral courage, self-reliance;
Never would stand up to the Southerners' defiance.

Vacillating, rudderless, increasingly erratic,
Stood by and watched as events turned more dramatic.

In 1860 the Democrats met disaster;
Split into two groups, Republicans were their master.

South Carolina right away announced its secession.
Buchanan by this time was in a deep depression.

He denounced secession but said he couldn't stop it.
Tried to resupply Ft. Sumter, but was forced to drop it.

Left all these problems for Lincoln to solve;
As a lame duck president, he couldn't get involved.

Went home to Pennsylvania, left political life.
Died alone in '68, never had a wife.

ABRAHAM LINCOLN
"Honest Abe"

Born in a log cabin on the Kentucky frontier,
Lincoln came from humble folks, hard-working pioneers.

They moved to Indiana, a placed called Pigeon Creek;
His mom taught him the Bible, the Will of God to seek.

He knew the scriptures well, could quote chapter and verse;
He never smoked or drank, saw no need to curse.

When he had questions, doubts and qualms,
He often found refuge in the book of Psalms.

From farming to business to politics and law;
His Illinois neighbors liked the virtue they saw.

They liked his sense of humor; they laughed at his stories;
They admired his honesty and his gift for oratory.

To speak like a prophet took courage and bravery,
With an evil splitting up our land, a system known as slavery.

The Fatherhood of God calls for the Brotherhood of man;
He said a House Divided could not forever stand.

With hope for the Union and faith in Almighty God,
He entered the White House, with his boys and Mary Todd.

Whether speaking to the people, or even the legislature,
He always appealed to the "better angels of our nature."

The shells fell at Sumter; he called for volunteers,
Not knowing that the conflict would last 4 years.

With North and South at war, would America turn to dust?
Lincoln placed on the coins "In God We Trust."

So many tough decisions, Abe often felt alone;
At times the Heavenly Father seemed mysterious and unknown.

The death of their son Willy brought agony and grief;
Lincoln's faith in Providence was his only relief.

Gettysburg, Antietam, Shiloh's devastation—
Was this God's curse on America: total annihilation?

Through bloody battles, mangled men, terrible travails,
The president said simply, "The will of God prevails."

The war to save the Union became a war for Emancipation;
Freeing the slaves would help restore the nation.

American democracy, the last best hope of earth;
A nation under God would see freedom's new birth.

He struggled with the purpose of this fiery trial;
When the war was over, could we ever reconcile?

After four long years of conflict and his reelection,
His second inaugural speech reached out to the Southern section.

"Fondly do we hope—Fervently we pray—
That this mighty scourge of war may speedily pass away."

"With malice toward none, with charity for all,"
For justice and forgiveness, he gave his trumpet-call.

He never lived to guide us through the just and lasting peace;
Killed by an assassin, days after the battles ceased.

"Now he belongs to the ages," a cabinet member said.
They laid his body in his tomb, but his legacy's not dead.

With the wisdom of Solomon and the patience of Job,
This rail-splitter's leadership was felt throughout the globe.

May we always remember Lincoln, and believe what he knew:
The judgments of the Lord are righteous and true.

FREEDMEN'S BUREAU

ANDREW JOHNSON

"Andy, Tailor"

He came from Tennessee, and though he never went to school;
He showed political skills, and was nobody's fool.

Apprenticed to a tailor, his mom taught him to read;
Championed the poor whites who wanted him to lead.

Elected to the House and later to the Senate;
Andy Johnson quickly made a reputation in it.

A states—rights Democrat in the Jackson mould;
But when disunion threatened, like Jackson he was bold.

When Tennessee seceded, he said "Not so fast."
Refused to leave his Senate seat; Confederates were aghast.

Lincoln made him governor, this loyal Tennessean;
The task for Southern Unionists at times seemed Herculean.

Rewarded for his loyalty in 1864,
Was named Lincoln's running mate to help Abe win four more.

The Union party won and he became vice-president.
Never dreaming he'd soon become a White House resident.

He showed up slightly drunk at the inauguration;
And then six weeks later came the Lincoln assassination.

Could he unite the nation after four years of destruction?
Was he the man to lead us in a time of reconstruction?

Southern states soon began to ask for readmission.
What would be their attitude, pride or submission?

Johnson's kind of mercy to the South was rather novel:
Their states could be forgiven, but first they had to grovel.

Terms for readmission would actually be lenient;
Southern leaders would be pardoned when he found it convenient.

He tangled with the Congress, the Republican radicals;
Their hatred of Confederates was downright fanatical.

The planters must be punished, the northerners would gloat;
They insisted that the former slaves get the right to vote.

Johnson tried to block them with the power of the veto;
Congress brushed him aside like an annoying mosquito.

A Civil Rights bill, Freedmen's Bureau extension;
Every issue, every veto caused more and more tension.

Push came to shove with the Tenure of Office Act;
His veto of that measure had a major impact.

To fire a cabinet member was the president's decision.
Congress said "Not unless you have our permission."

Stubborn and contentious, he wouldn't compromise;
A round peg in a square hole, he couldn't harmonize.

In 1868 Congress finally overreached;
For "crimes and misdemeanors" Andrew Johnson was impeached.

The case went to the Senate where his innocence was tried.
He understood he had the constitution on his side.

Vindictive Republicans came up one vote short;
They needed two-thirds in this kind of court.

Impeached but not removed, he became a lame duck.
Victim of circumstance, poor judgment, and bad luck.

Only six years later, he tried to make a comeback.
Elected to the Senate, his career was back on track.

His rehabilitation would be a major feat;
But alas he got sick and died before he took his seat.

ULYSSES S. GRANT
"UNCONDITIONAL SURRENDER"

He was born in Ohio, the son of a tanner;
Grew up to be a soldier, a military planner.

Through hard times and danger, he never said "I can't."
Common sense and courage marked Ulysses S. Grant.

Neither poor nor rich, just average middle-class;
Graduated West Point with grades enough to pass,

Married Julia Dent, raised four kids and some horses,
Served in Mexico with Zachary Taylor's forces.

He left the army for awhile, tried to farm, without success.
His family always helped him out when he was hard-pressed.

But in the civil war he proved he had what it takes,
To press on to victory, despite his mistakes.

At Donelson and Shiloh, he showed coolness under fire.
Who's this western paladin? men started to inquire.

Jealous generals and politicians criticized him out of spite.
Abe Lincoln just responded, "I can't spare this man, he fights."

Could we trust him with command? Wouldn't it be risky?
The rumors were he drank too much, he really loved his whiskey.

Lincoln laughed and said "Go find out his brand,
I'll send a barrel of the stuff to every general in the land."

Relentlessly efficient in this conflict titanic;
He always stood his ground, never wavered, never panicked.

From Vicksburg to Petersburg, the Union's best defender,
At Appomattox Court House, he accepted Lee's surrender.

The battles won, the rebels crushed, but bitterness didn't cease;
In '68 Grant ran for president, saying "Let us have peace."

A Republican administration, with voting rights for blacks,
The South was reconstructed, led by crooks and hacks.

Business made a comeback; greenbacks redeemed in gold,
His plan for St. Domingo the Senate thought too bold.

The Transcontinental railroad linked the east and the west;
Yellowstone became a national park, on the president's request.

Drove his buggy much too fast, pulled by a spirited horse;
Arrested on a DC street, paid his fine, of course.

Gave amnesty to Confederates, did favors for his friends;
That Whiskey Ring scandal almost did him in.

But he served two terms in office and might have had another,
Republicans picked Garfield, but could have won with his mother.

Ex-general, ex-president, his place in history secure,
Grant took his wife and family on a grand world tour.

Back home at last and fading fast, Grant's memories awoke;
Mark Twain published his memoirs so he didn't die broke..

RUTHERFORD B. HAYES
"RUTHERFRAUD"

He started his career back in Civil War days;
Republican from Ohio, Rutherford B. Hayes.

Studied at Kenyon College, then on to Harvard Law;
Had a righteous reputation; he seemed without a flaw.

Showed courage and leadership in the Union army;
A paragon of virtue, always forthright, never smarmy.

When the war was over, he went home to serve his state,
As governor and Congressman, Republican moderate.

But was the presidency an office he could handle?
Would he bring reform after Grant's many scandals?

The election of 1876 was the closest in our history;
The actual results are still wrapped in mystery.

Turnout was enormous; votes came in a flood;
The Democrats just knew they'd won, yelled "Tilden or blood!"

Three southern states sent in two sets of returns;
Accuracy and fairness were not the main concerns.

A commission was appointed to settle this dispute;
Senators, congressmen and judges of repute.

Eight were Republicans and seven Democrats;
When the votes were counted, Dem's said "Oh, you rats!"

Hayes became the president by one electoral vote;
But he had to sign a political promissory note.

Democrats griped for awhile, but then they closed their mouths.
Hayes ended Reconstruction, removing troops from the South.

Black folks lost their voting rights with no soldiers to protect them.
Republicans were banished with no voters to elect them.

In Washington Hayes worked for civil service reform,
A violent railroad strike caused a firestorm.

Chinese in California labored under no delusion.
Prejudice against them would result in their exclusion.

Hayes tried to govern honestly during all these events;
But he proved to be one of the most hapless presidents.

Had promised to retire after serving four years;
When he left the White House few Americans shed tears.

JAMES A. GARFIELD
"Boatman Jim"

Born in a log cabin, raised by his widowed mother;
Grew up in Ohio, named for his older brother.

James A. Garfield, amateur mathematician,
Civil War general, professional politician.

Worked on canal boats, the ones pulled by mules;
An outstanding student, he loved books and schools.

Went to Western Reserve, and then to Williams College;
A logical thinker, he acquired eclectic knowledge.

Knew Pythagorus' theorem, invented a brand new proof;
It really was a shame that he wasn't bulletproof.

Ambidextrous and brilliant, he had a skill unique.
With one hand he wrote Latin, with the other he wrote Greek.

After graduation, he went home to be a teacher;
Also did a stint as a Disciples of Christ preacher.

But politics was his calling, Republican his party,
With anti-slavery principles, enthusiasm hearty.

When the Civil War came, he joined the Union ranks;
Led Ohio volunteers, won victories for the Yanks.

Elected to the House of Reps before the war was ended,
Served through Reconstruction as the nation mended.

In 1880 Ohio named him to the Senate,
But as it turned out, he never served a day in it.

The question was for president, who would he endorse?
Garfield didn't know it, but he was the dark horse.

On the thirty-sixth ballot he gained the nomination.
Went on to win election to public approbation.

Four months later, he was inaugurated.
Four months after that, he was assassinated.

Shot in the back as he waited for a train;
His assassin Charles Guiteau later claimed to be insane.

Lodged in Garfield's back, the bullet escaped detection.
The president lingered eighty days, then died of infection.

The nation mourned his passing, struck down in his prime.
Quirk of fate? A tragic loss? Or was it just his time?

CHESTER A. ARTHUR
"The Dude"

A Stalwart Republican was Garfield's running mate;
An accidental president, turned out to be first-rate.

Graduated Union college, was Phi Beta Kappa;
Like fancy clothes, always looked dapper.

Though Chester A. Arthur went on to study law,
His rise in New York politics very few foresaw.

He knew which way the wind blows, he saw which way the tide turns;
He looked so distinguished with those muttonchop sideburns.

Boss Roscoe Conkling noticed, and took him under his wing;
Made him customhouse collector, as a patronage thing.

At the Republican convention, the factions compromised;
Half-breeds took the White House; Stalwarts second prize.

In July 1881 a half-crazed maniac
Approached Garfield from behind and shot him in the back.

Guiteau desired an office, to reward him for his toils;
Party loyalists just like him deserved political spoils.

The assassin never got his job as minister to France;
Suspended from the gallows rope he did his little dance.

But Arthur calmly moved to quiet the political storm;
Put partisanship aside and worked for reform.

He signed the Pendleton Act, important legislation;
Made more government hiring based on qualification.

He vetoed the bill to ban Chinese immigration;
Claimed it was unfair and a treaty violation.

Tried to keep the tariff low, but Congress favored protection;
Was interested, but not obsessed, with his reelection.

Vetoed a harbor bill that contained too much pork;
Finished up Garfield's term and retired to New York.

Dignified and honest, a model of civility,
Our 21st president brought needed stability.

GROVER CLEVELAND
"UNCLE JUMBO"

Though he never went to college, he passed the New York bar;
First Democrat president since the Civil War.

A New York governor, before that Buffalo's mayor,
Stephen Grover Cleveland was something of a player.

His opponents would sling mud in 1884;
Rumors about a love-child caused a mild uproar.

Never said he didn't do it; never said he did.
Never married Maria Halpin, but did support her kid.

But Cleveland's supporters had dirt on James G. Blaine;
That Half-Breed Republican rascal from Maine.

"Blaine! Blaine! James G. Blaine!
Continental liar from the state of Maine!"

More than just rumors, had proof which was better;
A document which ended, "Burn this letter!"

Republican partisans couldn't keep from yellin'
Dem's are for Romanism, Rum, and Rebellion.

Endorsed by the Mugwumps, committed to reform,
Cleveland campaigned and weathered the storm.

"Ma! Ma! Where's my Pa?"
"Gone to the White House, Ha-Ha-Ha!"

After all the hoopla, he became chief executive;
Served two terms in office, though not consecutive.

Portly but not jolly, he drank a lot of beer;
To all the office-seekers, he turned a deaf ear.

Uncle Jumbo! Nobody's Dumbo!
Didn't care for Gumbo! or Nativist Mumbo Jumbo!

He worked so very hard, nothing gave him such a thrill,
As when he stayed up late to veto a bill.

Fiscal conservative, believed in laissez-faire;
Vetoed pork barrel projects, hand-outs and welfare.

Scrupulously honest, integrity a must;
Said "A public office is a public trust."

Vetoed bogus claims for veterans' pensions,
The GAR complained, but he didn't pay attention.

Married Frances Folsom, she was only twenty-one;
Their wedding in the White House was dignified but fun.

Signed the ICC, for railroad regulation;
Tried to get the Indians to leave the reservation.

The Dawes Act offered a farming homestead;
Tried to convince them the tribal thing was dead.

In 1888 an old issue would return;
Reducing the tariff was his major concern.

Protectionist Republicans won that close election;
Gave old Grover 4 years to spend in reflection.

Returned to the White House in 1893;
Just in time for panic, unemployment, bankruptcy.

Stubbornly he supported the standard based on gold;
A four-year depression, who could have foretold?

He busted Coxey's army for walking on the grass;
His insensitivity ticked off the working class.

The Pullman strike was such a mess, whatever would he do?
Transportation paralyzed, but the mail must go through!

Sent troops to Illinois to operate the trains,
Union thugs and radicals cursed him, but in vain.

His popularity faded through his second term;
But his courage was undaunted; his principles stayed firm.

Retired to New Jersey, where his life began;
Pulitzer described him best: "He is an honest man."

BENJAMIN HARRISON
"Hoosier President"

Born in Ohio, grandson of Tippecanoe,
Moved to Indiana, grew up to be president, too.

Benjamin Harrison was successful in the law;
Changed careers for politics, like his old grandpa.

Served in the Union army, became a brigadier;
When the war was over, his ambitions became clear.

Elected to the Senate in 1881;
Supported veterans' pensions, like any Republican.

Criticized Cleveland's vetoes, campaigned for civil rights;
The goal of chief executive was where he set his sights.

Persuasive on the stump, his speeches strong and bold;
Face-to-face, one-on-one, he seemed aloof and cold.

In 1888 he was the Republican nominee;
The election was so very close, but he earned the victory.

Actually lost the popular vote, but gained enough states
To win the electoral college and send Cleveland out the gate.

His four years in office were somewhat uneventful;
Cleveland just bided his time; wasn't visibly resentful.

While Harrison was in office, new states numbered six;
Few issues were divisive in partisan politics.

Named as Secretary of State—guess who? James G. Blaine!
About his foreign policy, no one did complain.

The Pan American conference was a grand success.
More trade and treaties followed this, how boring for the press!

Signed important laws, like Sherman Anti-Trust;
Sherman's Silver Purchase Act turned out to be a bust.

But then McKinley's Tariff act raised duties to the sky.
Harrison said "never have wages been so high."

Ironic that he bragged about the nation's prosperity,
Right before depression hit with merciless severity.

Bankruptcies and unemployment mounted by the hour;
Voters turned on Harrison, brought Cleveland back to power.

Distracted from the campaign, his wife was quite infirm;
She died before he finished his single four-year term.

Went home to Indiana, practiced law and wrote some books.
Victim of the voters who "vote their pocketbooks."

WILLIAM MCKINLEY
"The Major"

Last president of his century, last civil war vet;
In temperament and politics, the most conservative yet.

William McKinley, clean-shaven, somewhat stout;
Faithful to his invalid wife, religiously devout.

Even-tempered if old-fashioned, cordial, patient, nice;
An occasional cigar would be his only vice.

Republican from Ohio, have we heard that before?
Don't bother getting too upset, there'll be at least two more.

Union army major, elected to the House;
Raised the tariffs much too high, the Democrats would grouse.

Governor of Ohio, protégé of Mark Hanna;
Popular throughout the North, from Maine to Indiana.

Ran for president 1896; it was a key election.
Democrats were heading in the Populist direction.

Bryan preached free silver, his oratory bold;
McKinley was for tariffs and a currency based on gold.

Bryan campaigned everywhere, carrying his silver torch;
McKinley stayed in Ohio, campaigned from his front porch.

His program of prosperity promised a "full dinner pail."
Bryan's plan for inflation was always doomed to fail.

Their decisive victory in eighteen-ninety-six
Brought Republicans dominance in national politics.

Mild-mannered but not meek, he didn't quail or cower;
McKinley's foreign policy made us a world power.

He looked with favor on Cuban independence;
The tarnished Spanish empire was losing its resplendence.

What would be the casus belli for our war with Spain?
The insulting de Lome letter or the sinking of the *Maine*?

The Spanish-American war lasted only sixteen weeks;
The US gained some islands, amid Democrat critiques.

Puerto Rico and the Philippines, not to mention Guam;
Became US possessions; our empire was "the bomb."

The Caribbean was our kiddy pool, from Key West to Aruba;
Free from Spain, but in our domain, the independent Cuba.

Was it a war of conquest, did we go too far?
John Hay at State said it was a "splendid little war."

Expansionist fervor ended U.S. isolation;
And then Hawaii was added by annexation.

With victory in the war and the nation riding high;
Economic growth seemed headed to the sky.

The turn of the century saw McKinley re-elected;
Bryan and the Democrats were once again rejected.

McKinley's second term ended the very next September;
That tragedy in Buffalo historians remember.

Following a speech, he shook hands with the crowd;
Suddenly two pistol shots made noise that was quite loud.

The anarchist assassin was immediately wrestled down.
McKinley lingered eight more days; then they laid him in the ground.

An honorable man, made the presidency stronger;
The murder cut his term short; it should have been longer..

THEODORE ROOSEVELT

"THE ROUGHRIDER"

Born in New York City to a family of wealth,
A skinny kid with asthma, they worried 'bout his health.

But fresh air, exercise, and lots of toil and sweat
Made him strong and taught him something he would not forget:

Winning takes effort in this world of toil and strife;
The life that is worth living is the strenuous life.

A patriot with love of country truly heart-felt,
The first modern president, Theodore Roosevelt.

Harvard-trained, his brilliant mind we can't overlook,
He was only twenty-one when he wrote his first book.

Politics to him meant public service to perform;
The New York state assembly saw him work for reform.

Republican progressive with a gift for oratory,
He had a mighty vision for our nation and its glory.

As New York police commissioner he went after the crooks,
In his spare time, he wrote some more books.

A rancher in the Badlands, he loved to ride and hunt;
A war with Spain in '98 called him to the front.

He led the Rough Riders up San Juan Hill;
Cool under fire, he showed courage and skill.

Americans loved their energetic war hero;
Elected him vice-president in 19-zero-zero

The very next year when McKinley was shot,
Destiny thrust Teddy into the top spot.

Youngest president yet, vigorous and robust,
He made a reputation as the man who'd bust the trusts.

This cowboy in the White House was wild and wooly;
The pulpit of the presidency to him was just bully.

He settled the coal strike with arbitration;
Made five new national parks, for wildlife conservation.

For the average working man, he offered a Square Deal,
Pursued big business regulation with Progressive zeal.

He knew a strong navy, a Great White Fleet,
Would make us a world power that couldn't be beat.

To help those ships sail from Atlantic to Pacific
A Panama Canal would be just terrific.

He preached and he bargained, he even threatened force;
His critics in Congress argued, uselessly of course;

They called him a madman, an imperialist lunatic;
He said, "Speak softly, but carry a big stick."

He showed Japan and Russia how to compromise,
And for his efforts won the Nobel Peace Prize.

Reminding Europe Monroe's Doctrine was no mistake,
He made the Caribbean an American lake.

Restless after two terms, he left Washington,
Toured Africa and Europe, but his work wasn't done.

Tried once more in 1912 the White House to regain,
Split up the Grand Old Party in the Bull Moose campaign.

Still seeking the lime-light when he was a fading star,
Asked Wilson for some troops to lead in the Great War.

Father of six children, a loving family man.
Author of three dozen books, a fine historian.

Integrity and virtue, a constant search for truth,
Were values he lived by, starting from his youth.

When he died at 60, the nation comprehended
They'd lost a great American, a leader truly splendid.

WILLIAM HOWARD TAFT

"Big Bill"

An honest public servant, without greed or graft.
A genial, gentle giant, William Howard Taft.

Born in Ohio, educated at Yale,
Republican workhorse, the party's Clydesdale.

Sent by McKinley, to the Asian tropics;
Administered the Philippines, his manner philanthropic.

Taught justice and fairness, respect for others;
He loved the Filipinos, his "little brown brothers."

Came home to serve as Roosevelt's Secretary of War;
Old Guard Republicans admired him from afar.

He tried to be a moderate, occupied the middle ground,
And took plenty of it, since he weighed three hundred pounds.

Teddy trusted him and picked him as his successor;
But Taft lacked the charisma of his predecessor.

Though elected handily in nineteen-hundred-eight,
To be a top-notch chief exec was just not his fate.

He cut quite a figure with his handlebar mustache;
But he never sought the headlines; his style lacked panache.

This heavy dude once gave the nation quite a yuck;
Replaced the White House bathtub after he got stuck.

At times he was ambivalent, at times indecisive;
His conservation policies were often divisive.

Ticked off the tree-huggers in the Ballinger-Pinchot tiff;
With his old friend Roosevelt it created quite a rift.

Frustrated the conservatives and angered the progressives;
His high tariff policies were seen as regressive.

His dollar diplomacy protected US trade,
Required all Latin American debts to be paid.

Broke up monopolies, brought suits against the trusts;
But he never got the credit; it was downright unjust.

Took a back seat to Congress; his own views seemed muddled;
Rough-and-tumble politics left him befuddled.

When Roosevelt made his comeback, the Republicans split;
Democrats took the White House; for Taft that was it.

Asked about the vote and losing his authority,
Said no one else became ex-prez by such a big majority.

Went back to Yale to teach law, his first love;
This job away from politics fit him like a glove.

From this academic chair, he didn't want to budge;
But then Harding appointed him to be a High Court judge.

Served nine years faithfully as chief of the Supremes;
His decisions were sound, never went to extremes.

A learned man with wit, jovial and merry,
He lies with other patriots, in Arlington cemetery.

WOODROW WILSON

"THE SCHOOLMASTER"

Born in Virginia, the son of a preacher;
Loved books and ideas, became a college teacher.

Erudite and scholarly, Johns Hopkins PhD;
Taught government at Princeton and then made history.

College administrator, governor of New Jersey.
Had politics in his blood, was drawn to controversy.

A persuasive speaker, a leader with strong views;
The presidential campaign was 1912's big news.

For twenty years prior, the Democrats were rejected,
But with the opposition split, Woodrow Wilson was elected.

His campaign promised changes, a progressive platform.
His first term was productive with a program of reform.

Underwood tariff, the Federal Reserve;
Under the Clayton Act, labor's rights would be preserved.

The FTC promoted business competition;
Wilson the academic was an effective politician.

Intervened in Mexico during that revolution;
Tried to stop the chaos, killings and persecution.

Sent troops across the border chasing Pancho Villa,
Occupied Vera Cruz, not a bad idea.

Wilson's foreign policy was challenged near and far;
The real crisis was in Europe, now aflame in war.

He tried to keep us neutral as the Germans fought the Brits;
Most everyone assumed that the French would call it quits.

His reelection slogan was "He kept us out of war."
But the door to our involvement he left slightly ajar.

The Germans with their U-boats sank merchant ships and liners;
When challenged thus Americans are fighters and not whiners.

The nation's ire was raised by the Zimmermann note,
A secret plan with Mexico that really got our goat.

Wilson asked Congress for a war declaration;
They responded quickly and started our mobilization.

He said the war would make the world safe for democracy.
But first we had to fight the kaiser's autocracy.

Always the idealist spoke of "peace without victory."
To our long-suffering allies, this sounded contradictory.

His Fourteen Points were noble, freedom for all nations;
But France was set on Germany paying big reparations.

After the armistice, Wilson traveled to France.
A program for a lasting peace he was eager to advance.

Negotiated long and hard, had to make concessions,
But did achieve agreement on his main obsession.

Countries large and small would form a world organization,
Dedicated to peace, called the League of Nations.

Came home with this prize, the Treaty of Versailles;
Opposition in the Senate rose and smacked him in the eye.

Republicans like Cabot Lodge had their reservations.
Wilson wouldn't compromise, took his case to the nation.

Exhausted by his speaking tour, he collapsed, then had a stroke;
Recovered, then continued the argument he provoked.

As the treaty was amended, he wasn't satisfied;
Without a 2/3 vote, it was never ratified.

Disappointed but unyielding, Wilson finished out his term.
Some called him stubborn, others called him firm.

Won the Nobel Peace Prize for his work at Versailles;
But the importance of the League he could never certify.

Isolation returned, to his great derision;
Perhaps it was the people's fault; perhaps it was his vision.

WARREN G. HARDING

"PRESIDENT HARDLY"

He came from Marion, Ohio, a newspaper man,
Handsome and non-threatening, a mild Republican.

Let's all "return to normalcy" after World War One;
No more grand crusades, let's have a little fun.

Warren G. Harding's style his critics liked to razz,
Began that bizarre decade known as the Age of Jazz.

The last year of his Senate term he became a dark horse;
The Party nominating him would later show remorse.

He stayed at home in Marion, a front porch campaign;
Celebrities came to see him; he loved to entertain.

Won in a landslide, beat the Democrat Jim Cox;
Women's suffrage made the difference at the ballot box.

Pushed by his wife Florence, who was much more ambitious,
He became the president, but his term was inauspicious.

He liked to get together with his cronies and play poker;
His ideas were shallow and his leadership mediocre.

He traveled to Alabama; made a speech on civil rights;
But Democrats controlled the South; elections were just for whites.

Didn't care for foreign policy, supported isolation;
Held a naval conference, never joined the League of Nations.

Aside from protective tariffs, he favored laissez-faire;
His attitude toward his cabinet was way too devil-may-care.

He made some good appointments like Hoover, Mellon, and Hughes;
But crooks like Albert Fall brought nothing but bad news.

Oil-rich lands in the west were supposed to be reserved;
Secretly Fall leased them, private interests would be served.

Directed the proceeds to his personal accounts;
Ripped off the taxpayers for huge untold amounts.

Where was Harding's oversight? Was anybody home?
This notorious scandal was known as Teapot Dome.

Of Harding's own involvement there was no evidence;
His problem wasn't graft or greed, just incompetence.

It was obvious to most folks he was in over his head;
And then before his term was up, the president was dead.

On a trip back from Alaska, he suddenly collapsed;
Died in San Francisco, of a stroke, perhaps.

Some suspected poison, rumors fell like rain.
Who might have killed him? What was there to gain?

No one ever proved any assassination plot;
Like most of Harding's presidency, that's likely best forgot.

CALVIN COOLIDGE

"SILENT CAL"

A modest politician, now that sounds ironic,
A New England Yankee, frugal and laconic.

Man of few words, compassionate conservative,
Of enterprise protective, of freedom preservative.

Born in Vermont, educated at Amherst;
If not the greatest president, certainly not the worst.

John Calvin Coolidge rose from rural obscurity,
Governed with wisdom, prudence and maturity.

A woman once said to him, "I made my friend a bet,
I'd make you say at least three words, or even better yet."

Coolidge didn't flinch when he heard this news,
Just turned to her calmly and replied, "You lose."

Elected to office in the Old Bay state,
Kept taxpayers in mind when he tried to legislate.

Told the policemen's union, when they took a hike,
"Against the public safety, there is no right to strike."

Named as Harding's veep in nineteen-hundred-twenty,
Untainted by the scandals, of which there were plenty.

Took over after Harding's death, purged all the crooks,
Cut taxes and spending to balance the books.

Progressives loved more programs for government bigness.
Coolidge said "The business of America is business."

Favored women's suffrage and laws against child labor,
Defused a minor crisis with Mexico, our neighbor.

Believed in property rights with utmost sincerity,
Presided over six years of solid prosperity.

Republicans tried to tell him that his work was not yet done.
But in 1928 he said, "I do not choose to run."

HERBERT HOOVER
"THE ENGINEER"

Born in West Branch, Iowa, lived on for 90 years;
His presidency a time of poverty and tears.

Educated at Stanford, a shaker and a mover,
Republican conservative, the Quaker, Herbert Hoover.

Trained in engineering, desired to serve the nation,
In World War I he took charge of food administration.

Humanitarian success takes skilled organization;
Hoover's plans and efforts saved millions from starvation.

Named to Harding's cabinet as Commerce Secretary,
The boom of the 'twenties seemed extraordinary.

Elected 31st president in 1928;
Despite his good intentions, his term seemed doomed by fate.

Fueled by speculation, margin buying, and cold cash,
The stock market boom collapsed in the crash.

Not just a correction, a slide or a recession,
The crash dragged the country into the Great Depression.

Banks failed by the thousands; millions lost their jobs;
Crowds of idle workers turned into angry mobs.

Hoover favored loans to help companies get on their feet;
He heard the cries of families who needed something to eat.

His Reconstruction Finance Corp was too little, too late;
His political support began to dissipate.

His predictions of prosperity often sounded lame,
For millions in those hard times, Hoover was to blame.

To make matters worse he signed the Hawley-Smoot bill,
With tariffs at their highest rate, foreign trade was nil.

Expelled the Bonus Army when their protest got too loud,
Still ran for reelection, bloodied but unbowed.

Lost in a landslide to Franklin Roosevelt;
Happy Days Are Here Again, was how the Democrats felt.

Hoover left the White House a defeated politician,
The nation's economy in an awful condition.

His presidential rating still ranks very low;
Could he have done better? Perhaps we'll never know.

FRANKLIN D. ROOSEVELT
"FDR"

He came from New York's wealthy class, his ancestry was Dutch;
His family had noblesse oblige; he had the common touch.

His hero was his cousin Teddy, that famous Roosevelt;
That Franklin might be president too was how his parents felt.

Enrolled at Harvard where he thrived, though not so much at studies;
Loved sports and student politics, and parties with his buddies.

Went to law school, passed the bar, but preferred to run for office.
A friendly and outgoing guy, not a bit stand-offish.

Elected to the state Senate, a progressive Democrat;
Campaigned for Woodrow Wilson, got a nice job for that.

Assistant Secretary of the Navy, (the post had once been Teddy's)
Franklin worked to build the fleet to keep our nation ready.

Stricken with polio, he suffered untold pain;
But he never let it conquer him, or cause him to complain.

His wife Eleanor encouraged him not to quit;
He never lost his vigor, his spirit, or his wit.

Ran for governor of New York in 1928;
Elected in a landslide to lead the empire state.

The very next year came the stock market crash;
Companies closed, men let go, banks ran out cash.

Months went by, production shrank, worse than any recession,
Millions of unemployed began to call it the Great Depression.

In 1932 restless voters wanted change.
To cast out Mr. Hoover didn't really seem so strange.

Roosevelt offered hope, reform, and a new deal;
A fresh approach, some miracle cures, to help the economy heal.

He loved to meet the voters, to travel and campaign.
Democrats were enthused; happy days were here again.

Won the first of four elections by a huge majority;
Restoring the people's confidence was his first priority.

He reassured the country, as he reminded himself,
The only thing we have to fear is fear itself.

Then came a flood of agencies, government alphabet soup;
TVA and NRA threw business for a loop.

AAA, WPA, the mind starts to boggle.
Was the New Deal a thought-out plan, was it a boondoggle?

The CCC put guys to work out in the National Parks.
Conservatives said the ideas came right from Karl Marx.

While Roosevelt charmed the people with his famous fireside chats,
Washington grew much bigger with thousands of bureaucrats.

To pay for all these programs, the government went into debt.
Prime the pump, the theory goes; "You ain't seen nothing yet!"

As the New Deal train rolled along, the Supreme Court tried to 'jack it;
Roosevelt answered the Court with his scheme that tried to pack it.

Congress never went along, the plan met with defeat.
But then the Court turned Roosevelt's way, he never missed a beat.

All in all the New Deal never worked the way it should have;
Business needed capital to recover the way it could have.

Then along came World War II, the nation mobilized;
FDR's pro-Allied stance at first was criticized.

Isolationists wanted us to stay out of any fight;
Though Hitler might drag Europe into a thousand years of night.

And then on December 7, infamy's darkest day,
Japan attacked Pearl Harbor; Roosevelt said they'd pay.

To punish their aggression and Hitler's bold defiance,
Roosevelt joined Churchill in a grand alliance.

He rallied the American people to endure the sacrifice
Required to beat the Axis, to pay the ultimate price.

A rendezvous with destiny this generation must keep,
So future generations may in freedom sleep.

From Midway to Iwo Jima and then the Philippines,
The Japanese were driven out by the navy and marines.

Resolute and optimistic was our commander-in-chief;
Defense of democracy his most devout belief.

He authorized Ike's invasion; the plan was launched on D-Day;
But Roosevelt never lived to celebrate VE-Day.

He died in April '45, victim of a stroke;
Men and women mourned him, both rich and common folk.

In the pantheon of great presidents, give FDR his place;
Surely Mt. Rushmore has room for one more face.

HARRY TRUMAN
"GIVE 'EM HELL HARRY"

In 1944 the Democrats took a leap,
Named Harry Truman as FDR's new veep.

A farmer/haberdasher from the Show-Me state,
Veteran, judge, Senator—a compromise candidate.

World War II was winding down; our armies were prevailing;
Roosevelt won another term, though his health was failing.

When he died, the nation mourned, then Truman took the reins;
Was the job too big for him? Did he have the brains?

His first big decision he made with aplomb.
To make Japan surrender, he dropped the atomic bomb.

With the Axis defeated, Mussolini and Hitler dead,
The question was posed, would the world turn red?

The Soviets' Red Army helped communists come to power.
Nowhere in Eastern Europe was freedom allowed to flower.

Truman announced his Doctrine in terms that were direct:
If the Soviets wanted trouble, then trouble they could expect.

Put Stalin on notice, US policy maintained,
Democracy encouraged and communism contained.

Gave aid to Greece and Turkey to stop the communist threat;
Warned against appeasement, lest anyone forget.

For European recovery, a huge new program began,
With loans and investments, known as the Marshall Plan.

When Truman made decisions, his message was always clear.
A sign on his desk read, "The buck stops here."

He proposed an alliance, a political hot potato,
Twelve freedom-loving nations, a little thing called NATO.

He told the isolationists, nervous nellies who were itchin',
"If you can't stand the heat, get out of the kitchen."

He sometimes lost his temper, but more often showed a grin.
He always kept his promises, like the one to West Berlin.

When Stalin blocked the roads, it caught Berliners by surprise.
Truman didn't flinch, but airlifted them supplies.

In 1948 he toured the USA by train,
Asked voters for another term in his whistle-stop campaign.

A Republican named Tom Dewey was his chief adversary.
Democrats rallied behind old "Give 'em Hell Harry."

The voting was so very close, election night so long.
The final count put Truman in; the *Tribune* got it wrong.

His Fair Deal proposals had trouble on Capitol Hill;
Raised the minimum wage; couldn't pass a Civil Rights Bill.

The Cold War heated up again in far-off Korea.
The communist aggression gave Truman an idea.

Let our response be strong, but through the United Nations.
Urge the Security Council to condemn the invasion.

Fought the North Koreans until his term was up;
Had to fire MacArthur; the guy just wouldn't shut up.

Truman took a lot of heat for this last unpopular act;
But left the nation stronger, and that's a natural fact.

He often wore bow ties, liked fishing and poker.
He served us well in world affairs, the nation's powerbroker.

Left the White House with his sweetheart Bess, went home to Independence.
His presidential reputation continues its ascendance.

DWIGHT D. EISENHOWER

"Ike"

Fought and scuffled as boy, played football, rode his bike,
Grew up to be a hero, nicknamed simply "Ike."

Graduated from West Point, went on to earn five stars;
Most brilliant of generals in that most terrible of wars.

Who was this gentle Kansan who destroyed the Axis power?
Became our 34th president, Dwight D. Eisenhower.

He strategized the landings of N. Africa, Sicily, and France;
Once on the Normandy beaches, our forces would advance.

Gambled on the weather, knew the stakes were high;
June 6 1944, D-Day, Do or Die.

A turning point in history, it sealed Hitler's fate;
Freed Europe from the Nazi scourge, its impact was so great.

The Supreme Allied Commander who defeated the Third Reich,
Was everybody's grandpa, a hard man to dislike.

His most impressive leadership in World War II
Made him a likely candidate when the White House came in view.

Democrats after Truman were madly for Adlai.
Republicans liked Ike, who beat Stevenson badly.

Elected 1952, made a truce in Korea.
Governed with restraint, a moderate idea.

Well-organized and tactful, knew how to delegate,
Non-partisan and fair, knew when to mediate.

His knowledge of the world, experience and maturity,
Made him the best defender of national security.

Could size up situations with insights so incisive.
Never panicked in a crisis, was calm but decisive.

Appointed Earl Warren to lead the Supreme Court,
Sent troops to Little Rock, black students to support

Signed that highways act to build the interstate;
Talked tough about the Cold War, but did negotiate.

Never trusted Khrushchev, or talked to him again,
After the Russians shot down that U2 spy plane.

Cuba under Castro joined the communist nations;
Before he left office, Ike broke off relations.

Presided over two terms of prosperity and peace,
The prestige of our country continued to increase.

Retired with his wife Mamie to a Gettysburg farm,
Popular to the end for his courage, grace and charm.

JOHN F. KENNEDY
"JFK"

Good looks, wit, and youth—what most folks remember;
And then that awful news on the 22nd of November.

Struck down in his prime by an assassin's gun.
John F. Kennedy's work had barely just begun.

Born in 1917 in Brookline, Mass.
Child of wealth and privilege, from the upper class.

Graduated Harvard, served in World War II;
The PT 109 affair proved his derring-do.

Saved his men from drowning, finally found an island,
Had little food or water, but at least it was dry land.

Asked about his heroism, Kennedy gave this quote:
"It was involuntary; the Japanese sank my boat."

Ran for the Congress, served in both Houses;
Married Jackie Bouvier, most glamourous of spouses.

Campaigned against Dick Nixon; the debates were on TV;
Showed intelligence and confidence, and youthful energy.

Won that close election by 100,000 votes;
Reports of false returns became historical footnotes.

Entered the White House as president thirty-five;
Youngest one elected; first Catholic to arrive.

Projected an image of humor, grace, and vigor;
His inaugural address called for moral rigor.

Promised the world we'd pay any price,
Bear any burden, and for freedom sacrifice.

Challenged his countrymen to serve their fellow man;
Ask not for a hand-out, but lend a helping hand.

His rhetoric was forceful; some actions not so hot;
The Bay of Pigs invasion—brilliant? I think not.

Gave Castro an excuse to ask Russia for some missiles,
Decorated Cuba with communist bells and whistles.

Young Jack announced his program, called the New Frontier;
Space exploration way out there and civil rights right here.

To stimulate more business, he called for tax cuts.
Sent young folks to the Peace Corps, to live in straw huts.

Appointed brother Bobby to a cabinet spot;
Their administration was known as Camelot.

Met Khrushchev in Vienna, the Russian was unimpressed;
The crisis over Cuba put Kennedy to the test.

Considered a bombing run, maybe another invasion;
Secret diplomacy, or the United Nations.

Settled on a quarantine, really a blockade.
Was Khrushchev's threat of war only a charade?

A nuclear stand-off, the world poised on the brink,
It was eyeball to eyeball, and the Soviets blinked.

Turned their ships around and took the missiles out;
Khrushchev gave in and sent Castro off to pout.

The Cuban Missile crisis was Kennedy's finest hour;
Though he sometimes seemed he was uncomfortable with power.

Made a speech for liberty at the Berlin Wall
But did his inattention lead to Viet Nam's downfall?

Earnestly desired to see schools desegregated;
Could have done more had Congress cooperated.

The people mourned when he was shot in 1963;
A nation lost its innocence in that tragedy.

LYNDON B. JOHNSON
"LBJ"

A long, tall Texan, grew up on a ranch;
Life-long Democrat, from the liberal branch.

Loud, brash, and pushy, combative, often crude;
Energetic, bombastic, politically shrewd.

Lyndon B. Johnson was larger than life;
Knew Lady Bird for 2 months, then made her his wife.

Trained as a teacher but turned to politics;
Led a New Deal agency at the age of twenty-six.

Elected to Congress, joined the naval reserve;
His party and his country he was always proud to serve

In 1948 he narrowly missed defeat.
"Landslide Lyndon" won a Senate seat.

His opponent contested those 87 votes;
They came from the graveyards, said some anecdotes.

Worked hard in the Senate, became its bellwether;
Was often known to say, "Let us reason together."

Asked by the Dems to join the Kennedy ticket,
Felt greatly tempted to tell them to stick it,

Was he second-rate, just a place-holder?
Who deserved the top spot? Wasn't he older?

Put aside his pride and joined the campaign;
Elected vice-president; never did complain.

The nation was distraught after Kennedy's death;
LBJ was quiet till we all caught our breath,

Then rallied the country for JFK's causes;
Urged Congress to act without delays or pauses,

Pass laws for tax cuts and for civil rights;
Give defense and space programs green lights.

Went even further with his Great Society;
Gave the Republicans high anxiety.

Declared war on poverty, didn't hesitate;
Added program after program to build the welfare state.

Medicare for seniors, a department known as HUD,
The stream of federal spending soon became a flood.

Trounced Barry Goldwater in 1964;
Signed a Civil Rights bill; said we needed more.

Government could do so much, providing guns and butter;
But Viet Nam made his administration sputter.

We had to stop the communists in Indochina,
Or dominos might fall from Taiwan to North Carolina.

From the Tonkin Gulf to the Offensive known as Tet,
We hadn't seen the end of the tunnel yet.

Half a million troops in that Southeast Asian jungle;
Did we lack the means to win or did Johnson just bungle?

Protests grew louder, casualty lists grew longer;
Johnson lost the will to fight as his critics grew stronger.

Announced he would rather not run for another term;
Viet Cong resistance turned even more firm.

Had gall bladder surgery, showed everyone his scar.
But what brought down his presidency was the Viet Nam war.

When he left office, US troops were still there;
Without a plan for victory, they didn't have a prayer.

Retired to his Texas ranch, he was glad to get back;
Lived another four years; died of a heart attack.

RICHARD M. NIXON

"TRICKY DICK"

He came from California, was driven to succeed;
Hated being second-best, determined to lead.

Went to Whittier College, then law school at Duke,
His rise in US politics wasn't any fluke.

Richard Milhouse Nixon, not content to practice law;
His ambition for power revealed his tragic flaw.

Stubborn and contentious, not a little argumentative;
When World War II was over, he ran for representative.

Congress was the forum for his famous investigation
That put him in the spotlight with his dramatic accusation:

A State Department bureaucrat named Alger Hiss
Had spied for the Soviets, used every artifice.

Hiss denied it all, but the evidence had him nailed.
Liberals were aghast when this Harvard grad was jailed.

With communists conspiring to undermine our nation,
Nixon's work in Congress helped make his reputation.

Elected to the Senate, then Ike gave him a call;
Would he be vice-president if elected in the fall?

Republicans won a landslide in 1952;
Nixon served two terms as veep; his public status grew.

Then in 1960 he was ready to go on top.
But JFK's campaign was too strong to stop.

Went home to California, lost the governor's race;
His angry outburst at the press was really a disgrace.

Moved to New York, practiced law for several years
While the nation in the sixties felt anxiety and fears.

Who would lead us out of these times of unrest?
Had we lost the Cold War? Were we second-best?

The Democrats imploded after LBJ was done;
Republicans told the voters: "Nixon's the One."

Elected 1968; his wish had now come true.
First on his plate was Viet Nam, whatever could he do?

Vietnamization was his term for cut and run;
Sent a message to the Viet Cong their war would soon be won.

Withdraw the American soldiers, do it little by little;
What happens after that? Nixon was noncommittal.

Bomb the North off and on, give aid to the South;
To make it sound more rational, use Kissinger's big mouth.

Start peace talks in Paris; travel to Beijing.
Such courting of the dictators could only mean one thing.

The anti-communist Nixon became the author of détente;
To bring about a peaceful world, give the reds what they want.

Make a trip to Russia; sign a treaty known as SALT;
If it grants a Soviet advantage, it's really nobody's fault.

Despite these achievements and a landslide reelection,
A cancer was growing, at first escaped detection.

A strange little incident, a burglary third-rate,
Became a huge scandal known as Watergate.

Break-ins and wiretaps, political dirty tricks,
Bribes and hush money paid by Nixon's sidekicks.

Senate hearings and court cases, stories in the *Post*;
Inside the Beltway, DC was all engrossed.

Nixon had his private conversations on tape;
Would these catch him in a lie or help him escape?

If the president was innocent, how come he didn't show it?
What did the president know and when did he know it?

Claimed executive privilege, found that in a book,
Told a skeptical nation, "I'm not a crook."

Stonewalled and withheld evidence, refused to budge;
Finally turned over the tapes, ordered by a judge;

Some crimes he had covered up, looking out for number one.
The tapes proved he was guilty; they were the smoking gun

Obstruction of justice is an impeachable offense;
He asked his friends in Congress if they'd come to his defense.

They told him it was curtains if it came to Senate trial;
Regretted all that time they had spent in denial.

Nixon's career then came to the end of the line;
Became the first president ever to resign.

Went back to California with his loyal wife Pat.
August 1974; let's leave it at that.

GERALD FORD

"MISTER NICE GUY"

It was a time for healing, for national concord;
For reconciliation, a time for Gerald Ford.

Grew up in Michigan, he was an Eagle Scout.
Friendly and athletic, religiously devout.

Played college football, then law school at Yale;
Served in World War II, then hit the campaign trail.

Elected to Congress in 1948;
His opponent, the incumbent, refused to debate.

Popular in his district, repeatedly reelected,
Had pals in both parties, he was solidly connected.

Affable, reliable, adept at befriendment,
Appointed vice-president through the 25th amendment.

Nixon was in trouble; Agnew had resigned;
What would the Watergate investigators find?

Enough to impeach Nixon and end his career;
Facts and public feelings made the situation clear.

Nixon's resignation led to Ford's takeover;
He said "Our long national nightmare is over."

In less than a month before opinions could harden,
Ford announced he'd given Nixon a pardon.

Democrats howled "There must have been a deal!"
Ford said no, it was done to help us heal.

Economic problems challenged his administration:
Deficits, joblessness, 12% inflation.

We can beat inflation, he said with a grin,
If we all wear buttons that spell the word "WIN."

Democrats in Congress enlarged their majority,
Ford accomplished little with his Republican minority.

Kept Kissinger at State, met with Brezhnev and Mao;
Said détente would bring us peace; didn't say how.

The loss in Viet Nam saw one final humiliation;
Communists rolled in during our chaotic evacuation.

The reds renamed Saigon after Ho Chi Minh;
Pol Pot murdered millions after taking Phnom Penh.

Don't blame Jerry for these Cold War defeats;
It would take a few more lessons to prevent more retreats.

He tripped on carpets, bumped his head a lot.
Two women tried to kill him, but they were bad shots.

Tried for an elected term in our bicentennial year;
Debated Jimmy Carter, uninspiring but sincere.

Seldom have the voters had such a feeble choice;
Finally the people spoke, if with a muted voice:

Let it be Carter, he has an honest face.
Thank Ford for his service as he steps down with grace.

JIMMY CARTER
"Peanut Farmer"

Grew up in rural Georgia, went off to join the navy;
Like many other southern boys, missed momma, grits and gravy.

Left the submarine behind, took over the family farm;
Friendly with his neighbors, he had that simple charm.

So James Earl ("Jimmy") Carter went into politics;
Southern Baptist Democrat, cracker from the sticks.

Elected as governor, served an entire term;
Balanced the state budget; his leadership confirmed.

Announced he'd run for president in 1976.
He'd need the votes of more folks than just the Southern hicks.

Told a cynical nation, "I'll never lie to you."
I'll do my best to finish what I specify to do.

Defeated Gerald Ford by two-point-one percent;
First man from Georgia to serve as President.

Gave pardons to draft dodgers, talked about human rights;
Worked hard in the office; stayed up many nights.

Had a hard time with Congress; he was an outsider;
Not a roughrider, more a chider and divider.

Perhaps his biggest challenge: how to fight inflation;
His energy policy was all about conservation.

His speech on the economy left us in a daze;
Blamed all our problems on something like malaise.

Thought it bad we still owned the Panama Canal.
Giving it away would be good for our morale.

His greatest success: the Camp David Accords.
Israel and Egypt got billions as rewards.

Loved détente so much he gave Brezhnev a great big kiss,
Was slow to realize that something was amiss,

The Soviets were planning another big invasion,
While Carter was caught up in the SALT negotiation.

The Russians crossed the border into Afghanistan;
Imposed a communist ruler, an Afghan yes-man.

Carter was perplexed, cut off the sale of grain,
As for the Moscow Olympics, our team would abstain.

Détente with the Russians: cold war tension's easement?
Or was it just a fancy French term for appeasement?

To make matters worse there was revolt in Iran;
The rebels there stormed our embassy in Tehran.

Took our people hostage, tortured them and beat them.
Carter said let them go, or at least don't mistreat them.

Tried to get them back; 14 months of negotiation;
The rescue mission failed, adding to our frustration.

After four years the nation had enough;
Replaced Jimmy Carter with someone seen as tough.

The problems of the seventies had put him to the test.
If he sometimes missed the mark, at least he tried his best.

RONALD REAGAN
"THE GREAT COMMUNICATOR"

The decade was the seventies, the economy was down;
With inflation and unemployment high, the nation wore a frown.

For months and months Americans were held hostage in Iran;
The Soviets were on the march, their troops in Afghanistan.

Our people were disheartened; our leadership was weak;
But out of California, a voice of hope did speak.

We could show the world that America's still strong,
That freedom is the right way, that communism's wrong.

He was a man of courage, a skilled negotiator,
With powers of persuasion, a Great Communicator.

An actor, yes, but never a libertine or a pagan,
A conservative with a vision, a man named Ronald Reagan.

Elected in a landslide, our fortieth president,
Took the oath and went to work, smiling and confident.

Iran released our hostages the day of inauguration;
Reagan then set out to lead a revitalized nation.

He said he'd make the armed forces second to none;
America's defense was priority number one.

Next he'd cut our taxes; with more to invest or spend,
Business would expand, the recession would end.

He called on the Congress to quit wasting so much money,
The welfare system didn't work; it really wasn't funny.

More resolute than Nixon, more popular than Ike,
He fired the PATCO workers after an illegal strike.

The nation held its breath when the president was shot;
But Reagan never once showed fear, instead he joked a lot.

His quips to the doctors gave them quite a yuck,
He said to his wife Nancy, "Honey, I forgot to duck."

Recovered in a month or so from the wound in his chest;
The challenge of the Soviets really put him to the test.

He called them the Evil Empire, his words and deeds were tough;
They called him a reckless madman; but he just called their bluff.

Put missiles in Western Europe to protect our allies there;
The Russians fumed and blustered that it wasn't really fair.

But Reagan knew that communism's days were numbered;
Their system simply fell apart while their leadership had slumbered.

With inefficient factories and technology so outmoded,
Their people grew frustrated as their economy imploded.

The Russians had to back down, come to the bargaining table;
Reagan proved himself in those talks, determined, calm, and able.

Refused to yield an inch on missile defense,
Let Gorby know we'd build it and spare no expense.

It was morning in America; in Russia the sun was setting.
Reagan's reelection had all the leftists fretting.

Nicaraguan Sandinistas feared he might invade;
Their enemies the contras did receive our aid.

Put pressure on the government, forced a free election;
The Sandinistas lost, showing communism's rejection.

The US under Reagan hit the comeback trail.
He led us back to greatness; he knew we would prevail.

Sent troops to Grenada, fought reds in the Caribbean;
Sent bombers to North Africa, hit targets that were Libyan.

Not afraid of peace talks, but willing to use force;
He knew we'd be successful, if we stayed the course.

His policy of tax cuts gave the economy room to grow;
The deficits got big for awhile, but then they got real low.

Despite his vocal critics and many a detractor,
Even Democrats had to admit, the actor was a factor.

When you remember Berlin and communism's fall;
Recall who said "Mr. Gorbachev, Tear down this Wall!"

So call him dunce or cowboy, a third-rate movie star;
But you've got to give him credit for winning the Cold War.

GEORGE H.W. BUSH
"BUSH 41"

Loyal Republican, devoted public servant,
Faithful father, family man, religiously observant,

Cared little for the "vision thing", his style was more pragmatic,
Kept his cool through dangerous times, events that were dramatic.

Governed by consensus, he nudged but didn't push.
An honest and a decent man, George H.W. Bush.

World War II pilot, graduated from Yale,
Showed good judgment usually, but then there was Dan Quayle.

Went down to Texas, made money drilling oil,
But politics was the field to which he gave his toil.

Served in the House of Reps, led the CIA,
Ambassador to the UN, had quite a resume.

In nineteen hundred eighty threw his hat into the ring;
Named running mate to Reagan, who took him under his wing.

Eight years as veep made him Reagan's heir apparent;
What you saw was what you got, his character transparent.

Campaigned against the liberals, used crime as a wedge.
Promised "no new taxes;" he would regret that pledge.

Elected 1988 as President forty-one,
The collapse of the Soviet empire had already begun.

When the Berlin Wall came down, Bush smiled but didn't gloat;
Millions in Eastern Europe achieved freedom and the vote.

Chinese student protest gave the communists a scare;
Crushed their demonstration in Tiananmen Square.

Bush criticized this action, but didn't cut off trade;
The outrage against China soon began to fade.

Attention turned to the Middle East and a tyrant named Saddam,
Iraq invaded Kuwait, Bush knew he'd have to bomb.

Formed a coalition of two dozen nations;
Threatened force would follow any failed negotiations.

Saddam was intransigent, kept his troops in Kuwait.
Set the oil wells on fire when forced to evacuate.

The "mother of all battles," Operation Desert Storm.
Could Saddam be overthrown and Iraq be transformed?

In four days of fighting, the rout was complete;
Saddam's armed forces met disastrous defeat.

Reeling from the blow, his army devastated,
Saddam was vulnerable, but Bush then hesitated.

Called a cease-fire, didn't march on Baghdad,
Left Saddam in power; the dictator was glad.

Saddam would survive to cause more and more trouble;
Had a strong desire to see the U.S. bombed to rubble.

Meanwhile back at home, times became tough,
Unemployment rose, the economy was rough.

The deficit was examined, the budget was appraised.
Democrats convinced George Bush that taxes must be raised.

This really didn't help him when ran for a second term;
His grasp of economics never was that firm.

Defeated by Bill Clinton, it was time for him to go;
Bottom line: Bush41 maintained the status quo.

BILL CLINTON
"SLICK WILLIE"

A president from Arkansas? Surely, you jest!
Bill Clinton was ambitious; he campaigned with zest.

Made a lot of speeches, ignored the worst rumors.
Got a lot votes from the baby boomers.

His background: Southern Baptist, with traditional Christian views,
'Long as they don't conflict with a feminist's right to choose.

Say, what's the big deal, this big ol' fuss with affirmative action?
His policy was approved by the Reverend Jesse Jackson!

Rescind it? Defend it! Mend it, but don't end it!

Said he might have smoked some pot, though he never inhaled;
Luckiest thing happened to him? Met Hillary at Yale.

His military record? Not much to say on that.
But he was a born-again, tried-and-true, New Democrat.

Just a left-wing conservative with some liberal dreams,
A moderate reformer, with progressive themes.

He tried to be a statesman, in the middle of the road,
Ivy League, Oxford man, in the Roosevelt mode.

Sometimes left, sometimes right, sometimes in the center;
It's hard to be consistent when you're government's reinventor.

But still the same slick Willie that Arkansas had known,
Sort of a Southern JFK, Elvis with a saxophone.

Didn't we need the government to make our lives better?
As for Monica what's-her-name, why can't we just forget her?

Gun control, a health care plan, a higher minimum wage,
Ameri Corps, school uniforms, Rush Limbaugh in a cage.

A 'nineties guy, so sensitive, he really felt our pain.
Did we really need to think about Saddam Hussein?

Signed NAFTA, welfare reform, and other Republican acts;
Congress nixed the health care plan, had to face the facts.

You can't trust Republicans, they're so mean and cruel;
They'd take away the lunches of little kids in school.

They'd poison the environment, cut down all the trees,
Lock up all the poor criminals, and throw away the keys!

Let business make a profit, give tax breaks to the wealthy?
All that money in private hands is downright unhealthy.

But the economy was strong, did better than expected,
Awash in union campaign cash, Clinton was reelected.

He traveled the world, visited every state;
Everywhere he went, he ate and ate and ate.

Our embassies in Africa and a navy ship in Aden
Were bombed by Al Qaeda and Osama bin Laden.

The FBI had done its job with Timothy McVeigh;
These other terrorist criminals we' d catch the same way.

Somehow the government deficit came under control
The budget was balanced, the economy on a roll.

He knew the American people; he took polls every day.
But some of those doggone rumors just wouldn't go away.

Then in 1998 a scandal was unleashed,
For perjury and obstruction, Clinton was impeached.

Acquitted by the Senate, he finished out his term.
To talk about his legacy makes many of us squirm.

GEORGE W. BUSH
"Dubya"

Politics was in his blood; son of president "Poppy."
Like his dad in many ways, but not a carbon copy.

George W. Bush, Republican from Texas;
His malaprops and syntax inspired the dyslexics.

But don't misunderestimate his popular appeal;
His campaign strategery was the real deal.

MBA from Harvard followed bachelor's from Yale;
Oil wells and a baseball team, which he bought on sale.

Thought he'd run for governor, against a gal named Ann;
Ms Richards ridiculed him and became an also-ran.

His tenure in Austin showed executive potential;
But still many wondered, was he presidential?

In the year 2000 he ran against Al Gore;
The veep from Tennessee had run for president before.

The election was so very close; Florida was the key.
Lawsuits over recounts brought more uncertainty.

Finally the Supreme Court said the recounts weren't consistent;
Ordered the results to stand, both sides had been persistent.

Bush had beaten Gore there by 500 votes;
Gore conceded gracefully, the Republic stayed afloat.

Once sworn in as president, Bush governed from the right;
Asked for a tax cut that the liberals said they'd fight.

Self-confident and outgoing, conservative but bold;
He seemed less compromising than the George Bush of old.

But his domestic agenda was stopped in its tracks,
On September 11 by those terrorist attacks.

Three thousand died on that fateful day.
Who planned that awful act of hate against the USA?

It was a Muslim Arab fanatic named Osama;
The world looked to Bush for the next act in this drama.

He said we'll track these terrorists and pursue them without fail;
We'll bomb their camps, fight on the ground, and We Will Prevail.

In only three weeks we had our troops in Afghanistan;
Cleaning out Al-Qaeda camps, fighting the Taliban.

The slippery Osama managed somehow to escape;
But a new and free Afghanistan would gradually take shape.

Bush was now committed to a long-term war on terror;
Not everything ran smoothly, at times he'd make an error.

But he put the world on notice of our determination
To stop the work of terrorist groups and their sponsor nations.

To the Axis of Evil he issued a warning:
Giving nukes to terrorists will bring your nation mourning.

That tyrant in the desert was heard from again;
The Butcher of Baghdad, old Saddam Hussein.

Worst killer since Pol Pot, making deals with the UN.
Stockpiling weapons, hoping sanctions would soon end.

Bush knew Saddam helped terrorists and wished our nation harm.
Laid down an ultimatum: Saddam must disarm.

To the weapons inspectors, Saddam had often lied;
Given time to comply, what did he have to hide?

Bush then did what his father should have done;
Sent troops into Iraq to stay until the war is won.

Democrats were ready to shove him out the door,
But Bush was reelected to serve another four.

What happened to the WMD our army couldn't find?
Was education really helped by No Child Left Behind?

When the housing bubble burst, would we all go broke?
Bankrupt banks too big to fail—was it just a joke?

Government bail-outs, the ever-rising debt,
Seemed to loom larger than the terrorist threat.

Bush served 8 years in office with honest dedication;
Let history interpret his impact on our nation.

BARACK OBAMA
"BARRY"

Forty-third man to be President
First black White House resident

Sports fan, family man
Used the slogan "Yes, we can!"
Sent more troops to Afghanistan
To fight Al Qaeda and the Taliban
Better watch out for Pakistan

Commander-in-chief Barack Obama
Sent navy seals to kill Osama

Finally showed his certificate
To prove his birth in the aloha state

Even-tempered, Mr. Cool,
Always did so well in school.

At Columbia, then Harvard Law
Classmates were filled with awe

Dreams From My Father, his first book
Made some pundits take a look

Chicago community organizer
Left-wing union sympathizer

Mainstream media's golden boy
Senator from Illinois

In '08 took America by storm
Hope and change, reform platform

Fight the recession with public works
Shovel—ready projects, jobs for clerks

Pull the economy out of the ditch
Build high-speed rail; tax the rich

End those long-term foreign wars
Instead let's build electric cars

Throw down a challenge, raise the stakes
Pass Obamacare whatever it takes

Never seems to get upset
'Specially 'bout the national debt

Unemployment eight per cent
So many houses up for rent

Problems simmer until they boil
Blame it all on Big Oil

Democrat with progressive views
Favorite target of Fox news

Eloquent, knows how to give a speech
Spending policy seems to overreach

The definition of erudition?
Or just another politician?

Messiah or pariah?
Great leader or bottom feeder?

Imbalanced budget?
How to judge it?

Leading from behind?
A nation in decline?

Re-elected in twenty-twelve
Judge his impact for yourselves.

Word